ALL ABOUT FANTASY CREATURES

DISCOVER
GNOMES,
HALFLINGS,
AND
Other Wondrous
Fantasy Beings

by A.J. Sautter

CAPSTONE PRESS
a capstone imprint

Blazers Books are published by Capstone Press,
1710 Roe Crest Drive, North Mankato, Minnesota 56003
www.mycapstone.com

Library of Congress Cataloging-in-Publication data
Names: Sautter, Aaron, author.
Title: Discover gnomes, halflings, and other wondrous fantasy beings / by A.J. Sautter.
Description: Mankato, Minnesota : Capstone Press, [2018] | Series: Blazers. All about
    fantasy creatures | Includes bibliographical references and index.
Summary: "In handbook format, describes the physical features, behavior, and habitat
    of wondrous fantasy beings"—Provided by publisher.
Identifiers: LCCN 2017002068 (print) | LCCN 2017014759 (ebook) |
    ISBN 9781515768555 (eBook PDF) | ISBN 9781515768388 (library binding) |
    ISBN 9781515768425 (paperback)
Subjects: LCSH: Animals, Mythical—Juvenile literature.
Classification: LCC GR825 (ebook) | LCC GR825 .S2753 2018 (print) |
    DDC 398/.45—dc23
LC record available at https://lccn.loc.gov/2017002068

Editorial Credits
Bobbie Nuytten, designer; Wanda Winch, media researcher;
Laura Manthe, production specialist

Photo Credits
Capstone: Colin Ashcroft, 28 (bottom), Collin Howard, 5, 21, 32, Jason Juta, 11,
13, 19, 27, Martin Bustamante, cover (left), 1 (left), 7, 15, 17, Mike Nash, 9, Stefano
Azzalin, cover (bottom right), 3, 4, 25, 28 (top), Tom McGrath, 29; Dreamstime:
Ateliersommerland, 23; Shutterstock: stockfotoart, cover (background), 1 (background)

Printed in the United States of America.
010364F17

TABLE OF CONTENTS

WONDROUS FANTASY BEINGS!

Many **myths** and fairy tales tell of wondrous beings. These stories bring elves, fairies, and others to life in our imaginations. What would these magical creatures be like if they were real? Where would they live? How would they act toward humans? Get ready to find out!

myth—a story from ancient times; myths often tried to explain natural events

BROWNIES

Size: 8 to 12 inches (20 to 30 centimeters) tall

Home: crawl spaces and attics in barns and farmhouses

Diet: bread, milk, cheese, porridge, honey

Lifespan: 600 years or more

Appearance: Brownies are small **humanoid** creatures that appear similar to rats. They have beady black eyes, pointed ears, and strong front teeth. Most brownies wear shabby clothing made from bits of scrap cloth.

humanoid—shaped somewhat like a human

Behavior: Brownies don't like to be seen. But they are very helpful. They often do chores for people at night. They don't expect payment but enjoy small gifts of food or shiny objects. If someone offends a brownie, it will respond by creating a huge mess.

CENTAURS

Size: 7 to 7.5 feet (2.1 to 2.3 meters) tall

Home: thick forests or grassy plains

Diet: meat, grains, fruits, vegetables, bread, cheese

Lifespan: about 75 years

Appearance: Centaurs are part human and part horse. Their human upper bodies are often muscular. Some males grow thick beards. Centaurs' strong horselike lower bodies are covered in brown or black hair.

arrogant—exaggerating one's own self-worth or importance, often in an overbearing manner

Behavior: Centaurs can often be **arrogant**. They think they're better than any other creatures. They normally avoid outsiders and work to protect their herd. But they can be loyal friends. They'll often help whenever a friend is in need.

Dark Elves

Size: 5.5 to 6 feet (1.7 to 1.8 m) tall
Home: large cities found deep underground
Diet: lizards, lizard eggs, rats, fish, mushrooms
Lifespan: **immortal**, but can be killed in battle

Appearance: Dark elves usually have red or yellow eyes. Very rarely, a dark elf may have dark blue or purple eyes. Most are especially good looking. They have slender, athletic bodies and pointed ears. Dark elves are best known for their dark skin and straight white hair.

immortal—able to live forever
raid—to make a sudden, surprise attack on a place

Behavior: Dark elves have violent lives. They begin learning to fight at a very young age. They are skilled with deadly weapons and magic spells. Dark elves often **raid** cities and villages to steal food, supplies, and slaves.

Dwarves

Size: 4 to 4.5 feet (1.2 to 1.4 m) tall

Home: large underground cities inside mountains

Diet: meat, potatoes, grains, fruits, bread, cheese

Lifespan: up to 350 years

Appearance: Dwarves have short, thickly muscled bodies. Adult dwarves have tough skin with lumpy ears and noses. Most dwarf men have long, thick beards. They often weave and braid their beards into fantastic designs.

Behavior: Dwarves are a noble and proud people. They don't trust elves. But they are usually friendly toward humans, halflings, and gnomes. Dwarves are skilled miners and craftsmen. Many warriors prize dwarf-made weapons and armor.

Elves

Size: 6 to 6.5 feet (1.8 to 2 m) tall
Home: forests and quiet mountain villages
Diet: fruits, vegetables, grains, bread, honey
Lifespan: immortal, but can be killed in battle

Appearance: Elves are tall with slender, athletic bodies. Their long, straight hair is usually blonde. A few elves have dark brown or red hair. Elves have pointed ears, bright eyes, and friendly, smiling faces.

Behavior: Elves are peaceful and respect nature. They enjoy poetry, music, and fine crafts. But elves can also be fierce warriors. Their weapons and skills can quickly defeat most enemies. Elves can be killed in battle. But they never get sick or die of old age.

FAIRIES

Size: 4.5 to 5 feet (1.4 to 1.5 m) tall in normal form

Home: woodlands with streams and meadows

Diet: berries, fruits, vegetables, flower nectar

Lifespan: immortal, but can be killed

Appearance: Fairies have two forms. In their magical form they appear as colorful flying insects. In normal form they appear as beautiful young women. Fairies all have lightweight **gossamer** wings on their backs. All fairies are thought to be female. Nobody has ever seen a male fairy.

gossamer—thin, light, and delicate

Behavior: Fairies usually stay hidden in their magical form. In their normal form they are friendly and outgoing. Fairies love nature and like to explore the world. They will often use magic to scare away anyone who threatens nature.

HALFLINGS

Size: 3 to 3.5 feet (0.9 to 1 m) tall

Home: warm, dry underground holes or small houses near rivers

Diet: meat, cheese, mushrooms, vegetables, fruit, bread, honey

Lifespan: 90 to 100 years

Appearance: Almost all halflings have curly brown hair. Halfling men don't grow beards, but some have sideburns. Halflings have large feet covered in furry brown hair. They never wear shoes or boots and can be very **stealthy**. They can move in complete silence to avoid being seen.

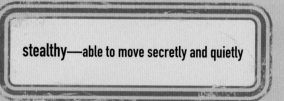

stealthy—able to move secretly and quietly

Behavior: Halflings are peaceful people. They enjoy good food and the comforts of home. But they can be tougher than they look. Brave halflings sometimes go on adventures. They face many dangers found in the outside world.

Gnomes

Size: 18 to 24 inches (46 to 61 cm) tall
Home: small caves and hollow trees in wooded areas
Diet: fruit, mushrooms, nuts, beans, vegetables, honey
Lifespan: up to 500 years

Appearance: Gnomes look similar to dwarves but are shorter. They have stocky bodies and strong hands. Males usually have long white or gray beards. A few gnomes like to wear pointed red or green hats.

Behavior: Gnomes like to keep to themselves. They have little contact with outsiders, especially humans. However, they are friendly toward fairies, elves, and others who respect nature. Gnomes are skilled craftsmen. They create some of the finest jewelry available.

MERFOLK

Size: about 7 feet (2.1 m) long
Home: warm tropical seas and lakes
Diet: fish, clams, oysters, crabs, shrimp, seaweed
Lifespan: about 200 years

Appearance: Merfolk are part human and part fish. Merfolk have **gills** in place of human ears. Their lower bodies resemble large fish with strong tails. Some merfolk magically change their tails into human legs to walk on dry land. But they must return to the water within 12 hours.

gill—a body part on a fish used to breathe underwater
territory—an area that someone claims as their own

Behavior: Merfolk don't like intruders in their **territory**. Merfolk may seem friendly at first. They smile and motion for human sailors to follow them. But they use this trick to lead sailing ships away from their secret underwater homes.

SATYRS

Size: 5 to 5.5 feet (1.5 to 1.7 m) tall
Home: forests and grassy hilled areas
Diet: fruits, vegetables, grains, bread, cheese
Lifespan: unknown

Appearance: Satyrs have the feet of goats while their **torsos** are similar to humans. Their bodies are covered in coarse fur. Satyrs' faces have several goatlike features. They have pointed ears, curved horns, and long whiskers on their chins.

torso—the part of the body between the neck and waist, not including the arms

panpipe—a musical instrument made of several hollow pipes of various lengths

Behavior: Satyrs love to explore forests and discover new plants and animals. Many satyrs are skilled musicians. They play magical **panpipes** to entertain friends or confuse enemies. Satyrs love big parties with plenty of food, music, and dancing.

TREEFOLK

Size: 30 to 40 feet (9 to 12 m) tall

Home: thick forests with many trees

Diet: unknown, but probably water rich in **nutrients**

Lifespan: 10,000 years or more

Appearance: Treefolk look like various types of trees. They have thick, trunklike legs and rootlike feet. Their arms and hands look like tree branches. Their skin is like rough tree bark. Some treefolk have beards made of moss or vines.

nutrient—a substance, such as vitamins and minerals, needed by plants and animals for good health

fortress—a place that is built to be strong and well defended against attacks

Behavior: Treefolk help guard and protect the forest. They move and speak very slowly. Some treefolk enjoy writing long poems and stories. However, angry treefolk can be fearsome. They are incredibly strong. They can quickly tear down an enemy's stone **fortress**.

Creature Quiz

1. Halflings are naturally:

   A) curious and adventurous.

   B) quiet and stealthy.

   C) loud and clumsy.

2. True or false? Elves live forever and can never die.

   A) True.

   B) False.

3. In the morning you find that the dishes are washed, but are not put away. You think brownies did the work. Which should you NOT do?

   A) Leave a gift of food.

   B) Leave a shiny silver button.

   C) Leave a note to complain that the dishes aren't put away.

4. Some merfolk can walk on dry land for up to:

   A) 12 hours.

   B) 12 days.

   C) 12 weeks.

5. Satyrs love to:

   A) craft magical weapons and armor.

   B) eat, play music, and dance at parties.

   C) spend quiet evenings at home.

6. Dwarves are not friendly toward:

   A) elves.

   B) halflings.

   C) humans.

7. A treefolk's favorite food is:

   A) honey.

   B) bread.

   C) nutrient-rich water.

8. In magical form, fairies might resemble:

   A) colorful butterflies.

   B) large dragonflies.

   C) both A and B.

9. Centaurs usually prefer to live:

   A) as part of a herd.

   B) by themselves in the forest.

   C) in small family groups.

10. Which creatures are known for creating the best jewelry?

   A) elves.

   B) gnomes.

   C) dwarves.

See page 31 for quiz answers.

Glossary

arrogant (AIR-uh-guhnt)—exaggerating one's own self-worth or importance, often in an overbearing manner

fortress (FOR-tress)—a place that is built to be strong and well defended against attacks

gill (GIL)—a body part on a fish used to breathe underwater

gossamer (GOSS-uh-mur)—thin, light, and delicate

humanoid (HYOO-muh-noyd)—shaped somewhat like a human

immortal (i-MOR-tuhl)—able to live forever

myth (MITH)—a story from ancient times; myths often tried to explain natural events

nutrient (NOO-tree-uhnt)—a substance, such as vitamins and minerals, needed by plants and animals for good health

panpipe (PAN-pipe)—a musical instrument made of several hollow pipes of various lengths

raid (RAYD)—to make a sudden, surprise attack on a place

stealthy (STEL-thee)—able to move secretly and quietly

territory (TERR-uh-tor-ee)—an area that someone claims as their own

torso (TOR-soh)—the part of the body between the neck and waist, not including the arms

Read More

Johnson, Sheri A. *The Girls' Guide to Fairies: Everything Irresistible about the Fair Folk*. The Girls' Guides to Everything Unexplained. North Mankato, Minn.: Capstone Press, 2012.

Sautter, A. J. *How to Draw Elves, Dwarves, and Other Magical Folk*. Drawing Fantasy Creatures. North Mankato, Minn.: Capstone Press, 2016.

Quiz Answers:

1:B, 2:B, 3:C, 4:A, 5:B, 6:A, 7:C, 8:C, 9:A, 10:B

Internet Sites

Use FactHound to find Internet sites related to this book.

Visit *www.facthound.com*

Just type in 9781515768388 and go.

 **Super-cool stuff!** Check out projects, games and lots more at **www.capstonekids.com**

Index